A Happy Christmas TO YOU.

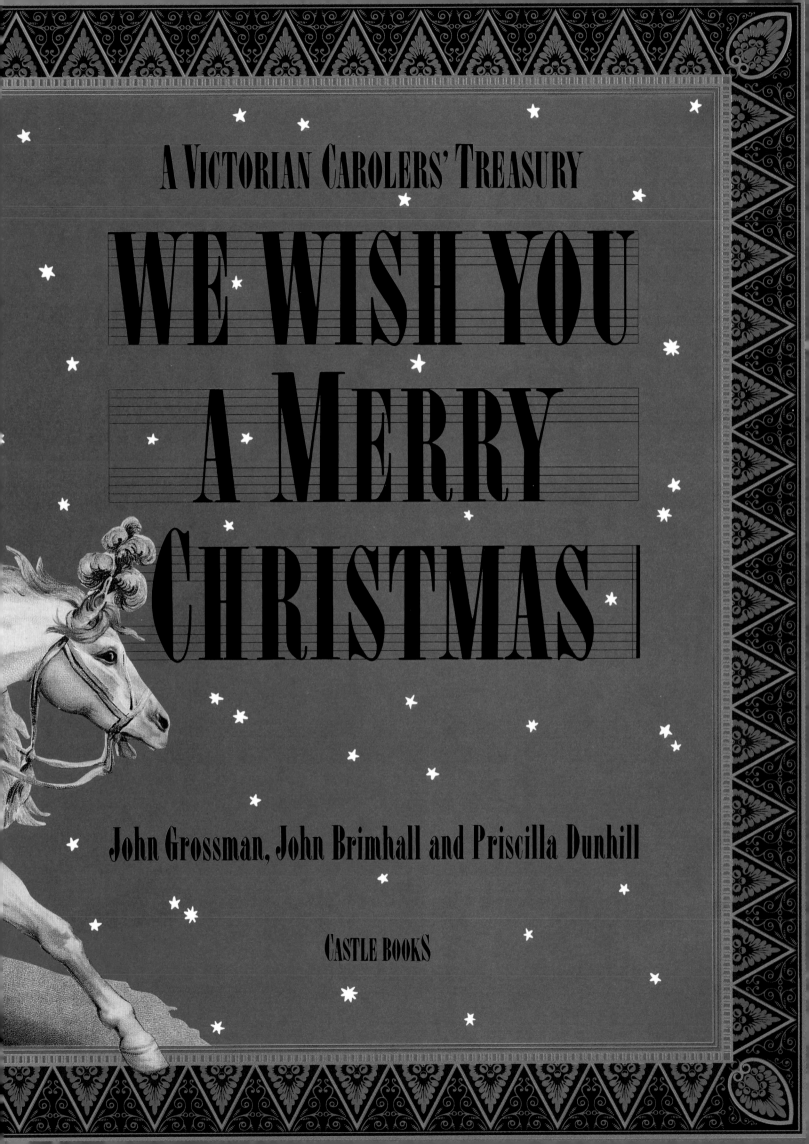

A VICTORIAN CAROLERS' TREASURY

WE WISH YOU A MERRY CHRISTMAS

John Grossman, John Brimhall and Priscilla Dunhill

CASTLE BOOKS

In memory of my mother, Ruth Howell Grossman, who raised six children during
lean times and still made sure that we all experienced the joy, magic, and meaning of Christmas so
everlastingly exalted by these old carols.–John Grossman

To my wife, Vergie Brimhall, whose support and inspiration made this a work of joy.–John Brimhall

I raise my cup of wassail to celebrate all those Sunday school and public school teachers,
aunties and especially my mother, Miriam, and my grandmother, Emma, who taught me the joys of caroling.
Sometimes we rendered verses in English, sometimes in German, sometimes
in Latin, but always we sung vivace.–Priscilla Dunhill

We especially thank Laura Alders, an exceptionally talented designer, for her many contributions to the final design of the book. Our thanks also to The Gifted Line Design Department: Julie Grovhoug, Production Manager; Jay Young, Macintosh Quadra 650 wizard; Holly Young; and Sean Arbabi, photographer. David H. Mihaly, Curator of The John Grossman Collection of Antique Images, made accessible the rare and often irreplaceable artifacts used in the book, while at the same time ensuring their protection. 🖎 The headings were set in *Mannequin* by Dan X. Solo, Solotype Typographers, Oakland, CA. Color scans were by ProLith, Inc., Burlingame, CA., with Iris color proofs by Desktop Publishing, Larkspur, CA. 🖎 For their help in the early stages of developing the design and production of the book, we thank Deborah Patterson, Toby L. Holden, and Thomas E. Dorasaneo. 🖎 Our many thanks to Bruce Kenseth for keeping the book on course and to Irene McGill and Carolyn Grossman for their vital support. 🖎 We are grateful to The Ephemera Society of America, and its president, William F. Mobley, for their work in preservation and appreciation of printed ephemera. 🖎 We thank Fred Smith of Maestro Music, Inc., Springville, Utah, for his excellent engraving of the music in this book; the librarians at the New York Public Library; and James Ashe and Pat Brandt of the John Jermain Library in Sag Harbor, N.Y. 🖎 We also wish to express our deep appreciation to Peter Workman at Workman Publishing for his commitment to this work and his vision of it, and to everyone at Workman Publishing; most notably, Sally Kovalchick, our perceptive editor, Paul Hanson, Sam McGarrity, and Nancy Murray.

Library of Congress Cataloging-in-Publication Data

We Wish You a Merry Christmas: a Victorian carolers' treasury / by John Grossman, John Brimhall, and Priscilla Dunhill.

29 scores with guitar and/or piano accompaniment
ISBN: 0-7858-1199-0
1. Christmas music. 2. Carols, English. I. Grossman, John II. Brimhall, John.
III. Dunhill, Priscilla

Printed in China

CONTENTS

INTRODUCTION

Carols have been sung in draughty castle keeps, in the great halls of Norsemen, amid the elegancies of Queen Elizabeth's court, in peasant cottages and on village greens, in soaring cathedrals and wayside chapels. In their spiritual power, carols stand alongside the stained-glass windows of Chartres, Handel's thunderous *Hallelujah* chorus and the sweetly pure strains of a Vivaldi concerto.

For at their heart carols are a jubilant message of love, a resounding cry of hope and renewal and rebirth. Sometimes the message is haunting and lyrical, like the American black spiritual "Go Tell It on the Mountain." Some melodies connect us to a deeply entwined pagan and religious heritage blended in Celtic and Gregorian chants or in the verse of the Norse blessing-song "Here We Come A-Wassailing." Often the message is full of grace, crooned in lullabies that celebrate the miracle birth of the Christ Child. And still other times the power of a Christmas chorus trumpets us right to a heavenly sphere.

Some carols are secular, such as "The Twelve Days of Christmas." Most likely this parlor song originated as a ballad, sung by troubadours who chronicled heroic epics of love and war in the banquet halls of noblemen. As they moved across France in the fourteenth century, the troubadors often incorporated the rollicking melodies of peasant ring dances into their ballads. The ring dance itself, called a *carole*, has ancient roots. In celebration of a harvest or village saint's day in early Europe, dancers linked arms and beat a rhythm with their feet or sang a repetitive refrain called the "burden"; the refrain carried the message of the song, a response to the stanza sung by the leader. From this basic burden-and-stanza structure, the medieval carol evolved.

Carols were also a source of discomfort to the straitlaced seventeenth-century Puritans, who viewed the singing of such joyful songs as disrespectful of their more somber traditions of religious worship. For almost two hundred years, unrestrained celebration was frowned upon in New England—indeed, not until the mid-nineteenth century, did the city of Boston even recognize Christmas as a national holiday!

Victorians, those ebullient nineteenth-century consumers of the Christmas spirit, wrote Santa songs and the irrepressible "Jingle Bells," pumping out the sacred and the secular with equal relish on hand organs in their Sunday schools and front parlors.

We inherit them all: three thousand years of jubilance and hope and joy, welled up from the wintry landscapes of human spirit. In a very real sense, these carols are entrusted to us—to pass along, to burnish, embellish or change as we see fit as they cross through our tiny moment in history. May you share in the delight they bring—and add to this universal voice of humanity.

In Joyful Celebration

So now is come our joyful feast,
Let every man be jolly.
Each room with ivy leaves is dressed
And every post with holly…
—GEORGE WITHER, C. 1660

"We Wish You a Merry Christmas" began its spirited journey in sixth-century England, when *waites* kept the night watch and with a cheerful tune sounded their message that all was well. Their songs still rang forth in the Victorian holiday season as village watchmen caroled from house to house, passing their hats for a holiday tip.

Celebrating the ancient ritual of festooning castle or cottage with greenery, "Deck the Halls" was set to a sprightly Welsh folk song. Greens were used to cleanse both household and spirit: pine boughs freshened the floor, pearly berries of mistletoe hung on doors warded off evil, bay and laurel symbolized peace. According to legend, holly was masculine and ivy feminine; in song, the words took new meaning. By the fourth century, Anglo-Saxons had assimilated the Norse custom of lighting a yule log, traditionally keeping a bowl filled with spirits as long as it burned. The *wassail*—both the bowl and the blessing "Be well"—is still observed in the English countryside, where Christmas bowls are filled with mulled ale, cream and fruit to welcome holiday visitors.

Isaac Watts began writing hymns at the age of fifteen. For the next sixty years, this eminent English theologian wrote hymns, fifty-two volumes of them, four hundred still in common use and none more revered than "Joy to the World." The present version of "God Rest Ye Merry, Gentlemen" blends the Celtic bard tradition of setting an epic story to music (so popular was this hymn in Victorian England that Charles Dickens incorporated it into his *Christmas Carol*). The hauntingly lyrical black spiritual "Go Tell It on the Mountain" was known and sung in the early 1800s, but not until the Fisk University Jubilee Singers took the spiritual on tour in 1879 did this poignant melodic story of the Sermon on the Mount become a treasured addition to the nation's Christmas repertoire.

We Wish You a Merry Christmas

Traditional English

Deck the Halls

Words: Traditional   Music: Old Welsh Melody

God Rest Ye Merry, Gentlemen

English Traditional

Go Tell It on the Mountain

Traditional Spiritual

Here We Come A-Wassailing

Traditional English

Brightly

1. Here we come a-was-sail-ing A-mong the leaves so green;
2. Bless the mas-ter of this house, Like-wise the mis-tress, too; And

Here we come a-wan-d'ring, So fair___ to be seen.
all the lit-tle chil-dren That 'round the ta-ble go.

Love and joy come to you, And to you glad Christ-mas

too, And God bless you and send____ you a hap - py New

Year; And God send you a hap - py New____ Year.

The Holly and the Ivy

Traditional

Verse:
1. The hol-ly and the i - vy, When they are both full grown, Of__ all the trees that are in the wood, The__ hol-ly bears the crown.
2. The hol-ly bears a blos - som, As white as li - ly flower, And__ Mar - y bore sweet__ Je - sus Christ, To__ be our sweet Sav - iour.
3. The hol-ly bears a ber - ry, As red as an - y blood, And__ Mar - y bore sweet__ Je - sus Christ, To__ do poor sin - ners good.

Refrain:
The ris-ing of the sun__ And the run-ning of the deer, The__ play-ing of the mer-ry or - gan, Sweet sing-ing of the choir.

For
thy mercy is
great unto the heavens,
and thy truth unto the clouds.
Ps. 57: 10

Joy to the World

Words: Rev. Isaac Watts   Music: Lowell Mason

1. Joy to the world, the Lord is come! Let
2. He rules the world with truth and grace, And

earth re - ceive her King! Let ev - 'ry
makes the na - tions prove The glo - ries

heart pre - pare Him room, And
of His right - eous - ness, And

THE ANGELS SING

Sing lustily and with good courage.
Sing modestly . . . Sing in time . . . Above all, sing spiritually.
—JOHN WESLEY IN *SACRED MELODY*, 1761

From the first angelic choir over Bethlehem, carols have been a joyous outcry of faith ringing down through the ages, revised and polished by a thousand voices, filled with the grace of commoner and king alike. The chorus of "Angels We Have Heard on High" traces its ancestry to the second century, when the Bishop of Rome beseeched Christians to sing out their faith in bold proclamation. In the 1700s, the devout Methodist Charles Wesley wrote his exuberant "Hark! The Herald Angels Sing"; an ardent champion of "singing out" one's faith, he published more than 4,500 hymns.

In 1818, on a snowy evening before Christmas in a small Bavarian village, organ master Joseph Mohr wrote "Silent Night, Holy Night" for two voices, chorus and guitar. The hymn was an emergency replacement for the music of an ailing organ that had wheezed to a final stop only a few days before. Captivated by its sweet purity, Tyrolean folk singers quickly adopted the carol and carried it with them over the Alps. Today the hymn spans the globe, translated into ninety languages and dialects.

Written by James Montgomery, fiery editor and one of the most beloved Moravian hymnists, the verse of "Angels from the Realms of Glory" first appeared in the Christmas edition of his newspaper, the *Iris*, in 1816. Set to music fifty years later, it gained great popularity in England, where it is called "The Westminster Carol." Adolphe Adam, a teacher at the Paris Conservatory of Music in the mid-1880s, was touted in London, Paris, Berlin and New York for his light comic operas and ballets—yet it is for the radiant "O Holy Night" for which he is best remembered.

William Dix, a Scotsman from Glasgow, was ill on Epiphany, the day the Magi visited the Christ Child. In the evening Dix arose and wrote the poem "What Child Is This?" Years later John Stainer, organist at London's prestigious St. Paul's Cathedral, set the verse to the poignant Elizabethan tune *Greensleeves* and assured its place among the perennial Christmas favorites.

Angels from the Realms of Glory

Words: James Montgomery   Music: Henry Smart

Moderately

1. An - gels, from the realms of glo - ry,
2. Shep - herds, in the fields a - bid - ing,

Wing your flight o'er
Watch - ing o'er your

all the earth;
flocks by night;

Ye who sang cre - a - tion's sto - ry,
God with man is now re - sid - ing,

Now pro - claim Mes - si - ah's birth:
Yon - der shines the___ In - fant Light:

Come and wor - ship,

come and wor - ship,

Wor - ship Christ, the

new - born King.

Angels We Have Heard on High

French Carol

1. An - gels we have___ heard on high,_____
2. Come to Beth - le - hem and see_____

Sweet - ly___ sing - ing___ o'er the plains.
Him whose___ birth the___ an - gels sing.

And the___ moun - tains___
Come, a - dore on___

in re - ply___
bend - ed knee___

Ech - o - ing their___
Christ, the___ Lord, the___

joy - ous strains:
new - born King.

34

O Holy Night

Words: John S. Dwight   Music: Adolphe C. Adam

Silent Night, Holy Night

Words: Joseph Mohr   Music: Franz Gruber

What Child Is This?

Words: William C. Dix   Music: Traditional: "Greensleeves"

1. What Child is this, Who laid to rest, On
2. So bring Him in - cense, gold and myrrh; Come,

Ma - ry's lap is sleep - ing? Whom
peas - ant, king, to own Him. The

an - gels greet with an - thems sweet, While
King of kings, sal - va - tion brings; Let

shep - herds watch are keep - ing?
lov - ing hearts en - throne Him.

Refrain:

This, this is Christ the King, Whom
shep - herds guard and an - gels sing.

Haste, haste to bring Him laud, The
Babe, the Son of Ma - ry.

rit. e dim.

44

Hark! The Herald Angels Sing

Words: Charles Wesley   Music: Felix Mendelssohn

THE CHRISTMAS STORY

No epic is more powerful, more full of hope, more tender than the birth of the Prince of Peace. Sometimes the story is sung communally, as it is in the resounding Latin chorus *Venite, adoremus* of "O Come, All Ye Faithful," chanted in early monasteries in the simple five-tone matins of the Christmas Mass processional.

The anonymous, sweetly beloved "Away in a Manger" springs from the compassion of Francis of Assisi, who deplored the stultifying scholarship that so deprived the Christmas story of its passion that peasants could no longer understand it. So Francis, humble son of a rich merchant who had taken vows of piety, built a crèche outside his small church in the mountains of northern Italy. Under a starry sky, parishioners watched the Christmas story unfold in song, enacted by real people and village animals.

By contrast, the buoyant melody of "The First Noël" was "borrowed" from a ring dance. With its simple repeated eight-measure theme, it was immensely popular in France, where it originated in the 1500s as a celebration of the harvest. The "ring" leader sang the stanza alone while dancers responded by clapping or stomping the refrain.

"While Shepherds Watched Their Flocks by Night" was borrowed from a translation of psalms published in 1696 by Nahum Tate, Poet Laureate of England. The excessive ornateness of the translation was defended by Thomas Jefferson, who declared that there was "nothing more moral, more sublime, more worthy of perusing." Tate's translation was ultimately set to music from Handel's opera *Siroe,* written in 1782.

Victorians avidly exhumed carols from ancient manuscripts, or wrote new ones in response to contemporary events as in the case of "It Came upon the Midnight Clear." Edmund H. Sears, a shy, rather frail Unitarian minister, wrote the verse on a bleak December day in 1849 when clouds of civil war already loomed on the horizon.

Phillips Brooks, crowned the "prince of preachers," wrote the majestically serene "O Little Town of Bethlehem." As a young rector, Brooks had visited the Holy Land—a popular spiritual pilgrimage of well-to-do Victorians, riding on horseback from Jerusalem to Bethlehem. Three years later, his journey became the inspiration for this exquisite hymn.

Away in a Manger

Traditional American

Tenderly

1. A - way in a man - ger, no crib for His bed, The
2. The cat - tle are low - ing, the poor Ba - by wakes, But
3. Be near me, Lord Je - sus, I ask Thee to stay Close

mp

lit - tle Lord Je - sus laid down His sweet head. The
lit - tle Lord Je - sus, no cry - ing He makes. I
by me for - ev - er and love me, I pray. I Bless

stars in the sky_____ looked down where He lay, The
love Thee, Lord Je - sus, look down from the sky, And
all the dear chil - dren in Thy ten - der care, And

lit - tle Lord Je - sus, a - sleep on the hay.
stay by my cra - dle till morn - ing is nigh.
take us to Heav - en to live with Thee there.

Christ Was Born on Christmas Day

Traditional

The First Noël

Traditional

Noël, Noël, Noël, Noël;
Born is the King of Is - ra - el!

2. They looked up and saw a star
   Shining in the East, beyond them far;
   And to the earth it gave great light,
   And so it continued both day and night.

3. And by the light of that same star,
   Three wise men came from country far;
   To seek for a King was their intent,
   And to follow the star wherever it went.

4. This star drew nigh to the northwest,
   O'er Bethlehem it took its rest;
   And there it did both stop and stay,
   Right over the place where Jesus lay.

5. Then entered in those wise men three,
   Full reverently upon their knee;
   And offered there in His presence,
   Their gold and myrrh and frankincense.

6. Then let us all with one accord
   Sing praises to our heavenly Lord,
   Who hath made heaven and earth of nought,
   And with His blood mankind hath bought.

JOYEUX NOËL!

While Shepherds Watched Their Flocks by Night

Words: Nahum Tate   Music: George Frederick Handel

It Came upon the Midnight Clear

Words: Edmund H. Sears   Music: Richard S. Willis

Slowly

It came up - on the mid - night clear, That

glo - rious song of old; From

an - gels bend - ing near the earth To

touch their harps of gold. Peace

on   the   earth,____   good   will   to   men,   From

heav - en's   all   gra - cious   King!____   The

world   in   sol - emn   still - ness   lay   To

hear   the   an - gels   sing.____

O Little Town of Bethlehem

Words: Rev. Phillips Brooks   Music: Lewis H. Redner

O Come, All Ye Faithful

Words: Frederick Oakeley   Music: "Cantus Diversi"

Songs About Christmas

What can I give him?
Poor as I am?
If I were a shepherd
I would bring a lamb
If I were a Wise Man
I would do my part—
Yet what I can give him,
Give my heart.
—Christina Rossetti

From the first touchingly humble gifts of the shepherds—a cruse of oil, a piece of cheese and fleece—the spirit of gift-giving has been an integral part of Christmas. Indeed, was not the Christ Child himself a gift of peace to the world? So fabled was the generosity of Duke Wenceslas the Holy, ruler of Bohemia in the 10th century, that he has been celebrated ever since in "Good King Wenceslas," the dialogue between the Duke and his page as they struggled through the snow to bring firewood, food and drink to the poor.

In "We Three Kings of Orient Are," Melchior, king of Nubia, brings a gift of gold symbolizing royalty; Balthazar of Tarshish, bears myrrh, a token of suffering; Gaspar of Chaldea proffers frankincense, a symbol of divinity. John Henry Hopkins, rector of Christ's Church in Williamsport, Pennsylvania, composed both words and music in 1857.

"I Saw Three Ships," began life as a ring dance. Over the ages seafaring folk added to and changed the verse. Sometimes the three ships represented the Magi or their gifts; sometimes, faith, hope and charity; sometimes the Holy Trinity or the Holy Family.

The impossible gifts of "The Twelve Days of Christmas"— "three French hens, nine ladies dancing and twelve drummers drumming"—suggest its patrician roots as a ballad. Victorians transformed it into an energetic Christmas parlor game, each of twelve players adding a personal "gift" to the rondal song and recapitulating each gift in sequence; participants who missed the sequence were out of the game, but added to the cheer by encouraging the others.

Good King Wenceslas

Words: John M. Neale   Music: Piae Cantiones

We Three Kings of Orient Are

Words and Music: Rev. John H. Hopkins

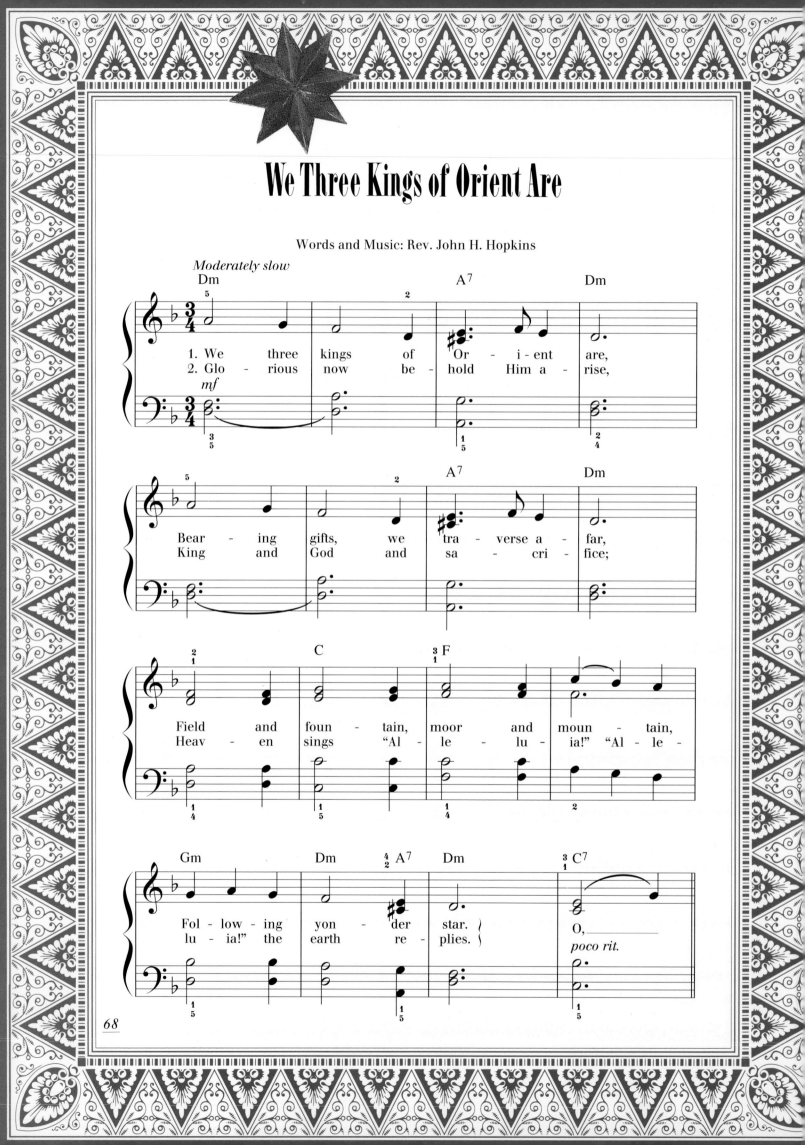

F · · · B♭ · · F

star of won - der, star of night,

a tempo

B♭ · · F

Star with roy - al beau - ty bright,

Dm · · C⁷ · · B♭ · F · C⁷

West - ward lead - ing, still pro - ceed - ing,

F · · · B♭ · · F

Guide us to thy Per - fect Light.

poco rit.

I Saw Three Ships

Traditional

Moderately

1. I saw three ships come sail - ing in, On Christ - mas Day, on
(2.) all the bells on earth shall ring, On Christ - mas Day, on
(3.) let us all re - joice a - gain, On Christ - mas Day, on

Christ - mas Day; I saw three ships come sail - ing in, On
Christ - mas Day; And all the bells on earth shall ring, On
Christ - mas Day; Then let us all re - joice a - gain, On

Christ - mas Day in the morn - ing. 2. And
Christ - mas Day in the morn - ing. 3. Then
Christ - mas Day in the morn - ing.

The Twelve Days of Christmas

Traditional English

SONGS OF THE SEASON

Our celebrated Santa songs—"Jolly Old St. Nicholas," "'Twas the Night Before Christmas," "Up on the Housetop" and "Jingle Bells"—are as much a part of Christmas as candy canes. The jovial, round-faced Santa whose girth shakes like a bowlful of jelly has charmed us in word and image, his jolly-cheeked countenance chuckling from street corners, shopping malls, in school pageants and advertisements.

Santa has not always been so. This legendary gift-giver wears many faces. Father Christmas in England dons a white or brown robe and has been known to become exceedingly tipsy while making his rounds astride a white goat. Kris Kringle in Germany dresses in black furs, giving out switches as well as sweets. Our Santa first appeared as a wispy elf in *The History of New York* by Washington Irving, who later depicted him soaring over rooftops in the snowy Hudson River Valley and dropping gifts down chimneys. Not until Clement C. Moore wrote "'Twas the Night Before Christmas" did the modern-day Santa literally take shape. Moore started the poem on Christmas Eve in 1822 en route with the family turkey when his carriage got stuck in a traffic jam. He finished it later that night and gave it to his six-year-old daughter Charity the next day. In the mid-1800s, Benjamin Russell Hanby used the poem as his template for "Up on the Housetop." During the Civil War, cartoonist Thomas Nast began illustrating the annual Christmas cover of *Harper's Weekly* with his "right jolly old elf" on a battlefield.

"Jingle Bells" has sent tiny feet and spirits flying for almost 150 years. James Pierpont wrote the perky song for his Boston Sunday school class to sing at their Thanksgiving program; when his class repeated the performance a month later, the song became a permanent Christmas holiday fixture.

Evergreen trees as symbols of renewal, celebrated in "O Christmas Tree," stretch deep into history. In the first century, Virgil described the already ancient custom of bringing gift-laden trees to Saturn, god of rebirth. Martin Luther installed a small table-size evergreen for his young son at Christmas, a custom brought by German Lutherans to colonial Pennsylvania. But not until Queen Victoria decorated a tree in Windsor Castle at the behest of her beloved German-born consort, Prince Albert, did the Christmas tree become fixed in the hearts of England and America.

Jolly Old St. Nicholas

Traditional

'Twas the Night Before Christmas

Words: Clement Clarke Moore   Music: F. Henri Klickman

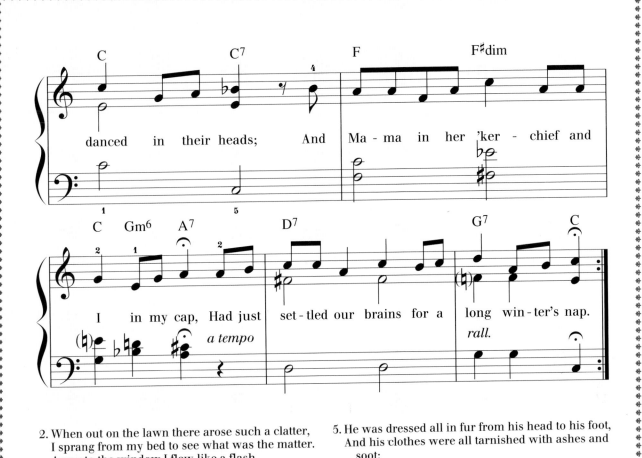

2. When out on the lawn there arose such a clatter,
   I sprang from my bed to see what was the matter.
   Away to the window I flew like a flash,
   Tore open the shutters and threw up the sash.
   The moon on the breast of the new-fallen snow
   Gave a luster of midday to objects below;
   When what to my wondering eyes should appear
   But a miniature sleigh and eight tiny reindeer.

3. With a little old driver, so lively and quick,
   I knew in a moment it must be St. Nick!
   More rapid than eagles his coursers they came,
   And he whistled and shouted and called them by
      name:
   "Now Dasher! now, Dancer! now, Prancer! and
      Vixen!
   On, Comet! on, Cupid! on, Donder and Blitzen!
   To the top of the porch, to the top of the wall,
   Now dash away, dash away, dash away all!"

4. As dry leaves that before the wild hurricane fly,
   When they meet with an obstacle, mount to the sky,
   So, up to the housetop the coursers they flew,
   With a sleigh full of toys, and St. Nicholas, too.
   And then, in a twinkling, I heard on the roof
   The prancing and pawing of each little hoof.
   As I drew in my head and was turning around,
   Down the chimney St. Nicholas came with a bound.

5. He was dressed all in fur from his head to his foot,
   And his clothes were all tarnished with ashes and
      soot;
   A bundle of toys he had flung on his back,
   And he looked like a peddler just opening his pack.
   His eyes, how they twinkled, his dimples, how merry!
   His cheeks were like roses, his nose like a cherry;
   His droll little mouth was drawn up like a bow,
   And the beard of his chin was as white as the snow.

6. The stump of a pipe he held tight in his teeth,
   And the smoke, it encircled his head like a wreath.
   He had a broad face and a round little belly
   That shook, when he laughed, like a bowl full of
      jelly.
   He was chubby and plump, a right jolly old elf;
   And I laughed when I saw him, in spite of myself.
   A wink of his eye, and a twist of his head,
   Soon gave me to know I had nothing to dread.

7. He spoke not a word, but went straight to his work,
   And filled all the stockings, then turned with a jerk;
   And laying his finger aside of his nose,
   And giving a nod, up the chimney he rose.
   He sprang to his sleigh, to his team gave a whistle,
   And away they all flew like the down of a thistle.
   But I heard him exclaim, ere he drove out of sight:
   "Happy Christmas to all, and to all a good-night!"

Up on the Housetop

Words and Music: B.R. Hanby

Brightly

Verse:

1. Up on the house-top reindeer pause, Out jumps good old
2. First comes the stock-ing of lit-tle Nell; Oh, dear San-ta,
3. Look in the stock-ing of lit-tle Will; Oh, just see what a

mp

Santa Claus; Down through the chim-ney with lots of toys,
fill it well; Give her a dol-ly that laughs and cries,
glo-rious fill! Here is a ham-mer and lots of tacks,

All for the lit-tle ones' Christ-mas joys.
One that will o-pen and shut her eyes.
Whis-tle and ball and a whip that cracks.

Chorus:

Ho, ho, ho!

mf

O Christmas Tree

Traditional German Carol

Moderately

O Christ - mas Tree, O Christ - mas Tree, How love - ly are your branch - es. O branch - es. Your boughs are green in sum - mer's glow, And do not fade in win - ter's snow. O Christ - mas Tree, O Christ - mas Tree, How love - ly are your branch - es.

NOTES ON THE EPHEMERA

Unless otherwise noted, all antique paper ephemera items reproduced in this book were printed by the nineteenth century color process called chromolithography.

Information about each item is arranged in the following order: type of item; title and/or description; size, where applicable; materials and printing method; artist, when known; lithographer, when known; country; date.

Descriptions read clockwise, beginning at the center top of each page.

Slipcover: Detail, movable calendar (holly); 9" x 17" open; six ribs fan out to reveal months; die-cut, embossed; 1908.
Songbook: Scrap (cherub with horn); die-cut, embossed; c1890-1900. Postcard (Santa conducting angels); embossed; S. Langsdorf & Co., New York; c1910. **J-card:** Scrap (two angels); die-cut, embossed; c1885-1895. **Book Cover:** Detail, movable calendar (three children caroling); 11" x 11"; five holly clusters and one star pivot to reveal months; die-cut, embossed; c1900-1910. Detail, stock advertising show card (Santa in sleigh); imprinted "Theo. Gier Co. Wine Merchants, Oakland"; 10 1/2" x 14"; die-cut, embossed; c1900-1910. Scrap (angel with trumpet); die-cut, embossed; c1885-1895. **Back Cover:** Scrap (three snow angels); 13 1/2" x 9 1/2"; die-cut, embossed; applied mica chips; c1885-1895. Detail, paper valentine (ornate scroll pattern); 10" x 8"; lithographed with gold ink; probably England; c1860-1870. **Endsheets:** Wallpaper pattern; 14" x 18 1/2"; machine printed; c1875-1890. Greeting card (children's choir); c1885-1895.

P.4-5: Scrap (Christmas tree); 11 1/2" x 6 1/2"; die-cut, embossed; c1885-1895; (children singing); 9" x 13"; die-cut, embossed; c1885-1895. **P.6:** Scrap (angel driving cart); 7" x 8"; die-cut, embossed; c1885-1895. **P.8:** Calendar (Santa holding toy pack and sled); 11 1/2" x 6"; die-cut, embossed; Frances Brundage (1854-1937); made in Germany; 1929. **P.9:** Details, postcards: (bear with ball); embossed; printed in Germany; postmarked 1909; (three children holding toys); embossed; Frances Brundage (1854-1937); printed in Germany; 1910.

IN JOYFUL CELEBRATION

P.12: Postcard (boy pushing girl on sled); embossed; "ASB" on verso; Germany; postmarked 1908. **P.15:** Postcard (children with tree on sled); embossed; "MAB" on verso; Germany; c1910. **P.16:** Children's book illustration, "Hanging Up The Stockings"; 10 3/4" x 9"; from *The Night Before Christmas*; McLoughlin Brothers, New York; c1896. **P.18:** Greeting card (boy carrying tree); c1885-1895. **P.20:** Postcard (children carrying tree and apples); embossed; Germany; postmarked 1910. **P.22:** Scrap (two children, family skating, sleigh riders); die-cut, embossed; c1885-1895. **P.23:** Album card (sleigh riders arriving at church); J.H.Bufford's Sons; c1885. **P.24:** Illustration (holly girl); 11" x 9 1/4"; c1900-1910. **P.26:** Greeting card (angel with holly garland); attributed to Ellen H. Clappsaddle (1865-1934); c1910. **P.27:** Detail, postcard (bell with holly and mistletoe); embossed; Ellen H. Clapsaddle (1865-1934); International Art Publishing Co., New York; printed in Germany; postmarked 1908. **P.28:** Scrap (birds on branches); die-cut, embossed; c1890-1900. **P.29:** Postcard (child holding toy bag and tree); embossed; printed in Germany; c1910.

THE ANGELS SING

P.30: Postcard (three angels with music); embossed; "SB" in circle on verso; printed in Germany; postmarked 1909. **P.32:** Postcard (angel holding fruit basket and tree); Ernest Nister, London; printed in Bavaria; c1910. **P.33:** Detail, postcard (angel holding rose basket); embossed; "EAS" at lower left; printed in Germany; postmarked 1913. **P.35:** Scrap (angel trio); die-cut, embossed; c1900-1910. **P.36:** Postcard (two angels); Germany; postmarked 1906. **P.37:** Scrap (two angels); die-cut, embossed; c1885-1895. **P.38:** Scrap (children dancing); die-cut, embossed; c1890-1900. **P.39:** Scrap (house in snow); die-cut, embossed; c1890-1900. **P.40:** Postcard (child holding candles); embossed; "EAS" at lower left; printed in Germany; c1910. **P.41:** Detail, postcard (two angels singing); Raphael Tuck & Sons, London; chromographed in Prussia; postmarked 1903. **P.42:** Postcard (nativity scene); embossed; Paul

Finkenrath, Berlin; printed in Germany; postmarked 1910. **P.43:** Scrap (angel holding garland); die-cut, embossed; c1885-1895. **P.44:** Scrap (winter scene); die-cut, embossed; c1885-1895. **P.45:** Postcard (Christ Child with two angels); embossed; "MAB" on verso; printed in Germany; 1911. **P.46:** Scrap (angel blowing horn); die-cut, embossed; c1885-1895. **P.47:** Scrap (dove with rose); die-cut, embossed; c1890-1900.

THE CHRISTMAS STORY

P.48: Scrap (children playing with toys); 13" x 9 1/4"; die-cut, embossed; c1885-1895. Detail, paper valentine (ornate scroll pattern); 10" x 8"; lithographed with gold ink; probably England; c1860-1870. **P.50:** Postcard (nativity scene); embossed; printed in Germany; postmarked 1909. **P.51:** Scrap (nativity scene); die-cut, embossed; c1885-1895. Detail, postcard (three kings); embossed; printed in Germany; postmarked 1915. **P.52:** Postcard (children admiring tree); Raphael Tuck & Sons, London; printed in Berlin; inscribed 1906. **P.53:** Postcard (two angels singing); embossed; International Art Publishing Co., New York; c1905. **P.55:** Postcard (angel portrait); embossed; Paul Finkenrath, Berlin; c1910. **P.56:** Postcard (nativity scene); Ernest Nister, London; printed in Bavaria; c1910. **P.57:** Scrap (sheep); die-cut, embossed; c1890-1900. **P.58-59:** Flat Dresden ornaments (stars); gold and red foil over cardboard, flashed, embossed; Germany; c1900. **P.60:** Postcard (three kings approaching Bethlehem); embossed; printed in Germany; c1910. **P.61:** Detail, uncut scrap sheet (Mary with Christ Child); 8 1/2" x 11"; die-cut, embossed; c1885-1895. **P.63:** Paper dolls (four choir members); die-cut, embossed, easel-back; c1890-1900.

SONGS ABOUT CHRISTMAS

P.64: Postcard (boy and dog on steps); embossed; "MAB" on verso; printed in Germany; postmarked 1915; **P.66:** Postcard (Santa holding toys and staff); embossed; c1910. **P.68-69:** Flat Dresden ornaments (stars); gold foil over cardboard, flashed, embossed; Germany; c1900. **P.69:** Postcard (three kings bearing gifts); "SB" on verso; printed in Germany; postmarked 1921. **P.70:** Detail, postcard (bells with holly and mistletoe); embossed; Ellen H. Clapsaddle (1865-1934); International Art Publishing Co., New York; printed in Germany; postmarked 1908. Scrap (children pulling sleigh); 5" x 5 1/2"; die-cut, embossed; c1885-1895. **P.71:** Album card (child holding holly); applied red and green mica chips; c1880-1890. **P.72:** Postcard (child carrying gifts); embossed; Ellen H. Clapsaddle (1865-1934); International Art Publishing Co., New York; printed in Germany; c1910. **P.73:** Detail, postcard (teddy bear driving cart); embossed; Ellen H. Clapsaddle (1865-1934); International Art Publishing Co., New York; printed in Germany; postmarked 1908. **P.74-75:** Detail, greeting card (children dancing); c1885-1895. **P.76:** Scrap (pine boughs); die-cut, embossed; c1890-1900. **P.77:** Postcard (couple kissing); embossed; Germany; postmarked 1910.

SONGS OF THE SEASON

P.78: Scrap (Santa holding tree and toys); 12" x 7 1/2"; die-cut, embossed; c1885-1895; Detail, paper valentine (ornate scroll pattern); 10" x 8"; lithographed with gold ink; probably England; c1860-1870. **P.80:** Trade card (children telephoning Santa); 6 3/8" x 5 3/8"; Hills Brothers' Fine Coffees advertisement on verso; Louis Prang & Co., Boston; 1886. **P.81:** Detail, greeting card (girl holding toys); c1900-1910. **P.83:** Detail, album card (dressed male mouse); c1875-1885. Detail, postcard (dancing mice); embossed; Germany; c1905. Detail, album card (dressed female mouse); c1875-1885. **P.84-85:** Children's book illustration (Santa flying in sleigh); 12 1/4" x 19 1/2"; from *The Night Before Christmas*; McLoughlin Brothers, New York; c1896. **P.86:** Details, postcards: (filled stocking); embossed; Ellen H. Clapsaddle (1865-1934); printed in Germany; c1910; (puppy); embossed; Ellen H. Clapsaddle (1865-1934); International Art Publishing Co., New York; printed in Germany; c1910. **P.87:** Children's book illustration, "On The Chimney Top"; 10 3/4" x 9"; from *The Night Before Christmas*; McLoughlin Brothers, New York; c1896. **P.88-89:** Scrap (holly with bells); die-cut, embossed; c1885-1895. **P.90:** Scrap (Christmas tree); 13" x 8 1/2"; die-cut, embossed; c1885-1895. Detail, paper valentine (ornate scroll pattern); 10" x 8"; lithographed with gold ink; probably England; c1860-1870. **P.91:** Dimensional Dresden ornament (heart candy container); paper over cardboard, linen-lined, drawstring; Germany; c1900. **P.92-93:** Scrap (girl holding gifts, boy holding gifts); 12" x 5 1/2"; die-cut, embossed; printed in Germany; c1900-1910.